True-Life Pirates

Black Bart Roberts

Cavendish Square

New York

Laura L. Sullivan

Published in 2015 by Cavendish Square Publishing, LLC
243 5th Avenue, Suite 136, New York, NY 10016

Library of Congress Cataloging-in-Publication Data

Sullivan, Laura L., 1974-
Black Bart Roberts / Laura L. Sullivan.
pages cm. — (True life pirates)
Includes bibliographical references and index.
ISBN 978-1-50260-207-7 (hardcover) ISBN 978-1-50260-206-0 (ebook)
1. Roberts, Bartholomew, 1682?-1722—Juvenile literature. 2. Pirates—Wales—Biography—Juvenile literature. I. Title.

G537.R74S85 2015
910.4'5—dc23
[B]

2014022792

Editorial Director: David McNamara
Editor: Andrew Coddington
Copy Editor: Cynthia Roby
Art Director: Jeffrey Talbot

Senior Designer: Amy Greenan
Senior Production Manager: Jennifer Ryder-Talbot
Production Editor: Sam Cochrane
Photo Research: J8 Media

Printed in the United States of America

Contents

1 The Dread Pirate Roberts 5

2 From Cabin Boy to Captain 13

3 The Most Successful Pirate in History . . 23

4 The End of Black Bart 33

Timeline 40

Glossary 42

Find Out More 44

Bibliography 46

Index 47

About the Author 48

one

The Dread Pirate Roberts

Some people describe Bartholomew Roberts, also known as Black Bart, as a ruthless **pirate**. Others consider him a **pragmatist**, who was only violent when he felt it necessary. The truth of his personality might be somewhere in between. What we do know for sure is that his actions often show him in a terrible light. One event in particular has branded him forever as one of the cruelest pirates in history.

In January 1722, Roberts had just finished a long bout of **pillaging** along the Atlantic coast of Africa. After relaxing on an island and repairing their ships, he and his crew were ready to resume their piracy.

Pirate captain Bartholomew Roberts was one of the most successful buccaneers to sail the seas.

They sailed into the harbor of Whydah (also known as Ouidah), a town active in the slave trade on the coast of what is now Benin. Roberts came across eleven ships at anchor. Their captains and crew were all ashore negotiating the purchase of slaves.

By that point in his career, Roberts was so notorious that as soon as he identified himself, ten of those ships surrendered right away. Roberts used his fame to make an easy fortune. He didn't always bother actually attacking ships. Fighting put him, his crew, and his own vessels at risk. Like most of the world's top predators, he preferred to save his strength and win simply by the intimidation of his reputation. He could just sail into view, demand a payoff, and sail away again, safe and rich. In Whydah harbor he collected 8 pounds (3.6 kilograms) of gold dust from each of the ten captains. The eleventh, though, refused to pay.

Captain Fletcher was in charge of the slave ship *Porcupine*. He and his crew were safely on shore, having already purchased and loaded some eighty slaves onto the ship. As soon as Fletcher sent back an arrogant message stating that he refused to make deals with pirates, Roberts ordered his men to row over to the *Porcupine*, set the slaves free, and set fire to the ship.

For reasons unknown, Roberts's order was changed during the raid and the results were deadly. It may have been that the other captains were organizing resistance. It might also have been that the pirates spotted British navy sails approaching the harbor, and Roberts decided he had to flee sooner than expected. Maybe it wasn't even his decision,

After first beginning to set the slaves aboard the *Porcupine* free, Roberts's crew decided to instead set fire to the ship while many of the slaves were still shackled.

but that his crew simply didn't follow his orders. Whatever the reason, the pirates found that unshackling the slaves was taking much longer than expected, so they set fire to the ship right away. All of the slaves who remained chained either to the ship or to each other were burned to death. The ones who had been unshackled jumped overboard to escape the flames and were quickly torn apart by the sharks that haunted the harbor. None of the slaves survived.

This terrible deed was to be one of Roberts's final acts of piracy. At that time, the British navy had been stalking Roberts for weeks, and they would catch up with him soon. Though Roberts's disregard for human life will always be remembered, he was a complicated man who seemed to always have had mixed feelings about being a pirate.

Black Bart

Bartholomew Roberts today is known by the nickname "Black Bart." He was never called by that name during his lifetime, as far as we know. The name wasn't inspired by his villainous character, but rather by his appearance. He is described as a tall black man. In the eighteenth century, "black" was used to refer to hair and eye color more than skin color. Because he was from Wales, his nickname is often given in Welsh: *Barti Ddu.*

The End of the Golden Age

Roberts's piratical career started during the final years of the **Golden Age of Piracy**. That era of plundering the high seas had begun its grand finale with the death of the notorious Blackbeard a few years before Roberts got started. Blackbeard was the best known of the dozens of pirate captains, and around 1,500 to 2,000 pirate crew, who pillaged villages and captured ships in the Caribbean and along the North American Atlantic coast. Other famous pirates of the time just before Roberts took to piracy include Charles Vane, Stede Bonnet, Calico Jack Rackham, and two notorious female pirates, Anne Bonny and Mary Read.

Piracy had flourished in the period immediately following Queen Anne's War, a conflict between France and England over which nation would ultimately control North America. Many Royal Navy ships prowled the Caribbean waters, while **privateers** were commissioned to harass enemy vessels, and merchant ships provided supplies to the combatants. When a peace treaty was signed in 1713, many of those experienced sailors were suddenly unemployed. They had all the skills of able seaman, but with reduced demand for sailors they had no way to make money—no legal way, that is. Many of them turned to piracy.

The increase in trade across the Atlantic meant that there were plenty of targets for would-be pirates. Unlike in previous decades, few of the vessels were Spanish treasure ships full of gold and jewels from South America. Most were merchant ships that were part of the **triangular slave trade.** In that system, manufactured goods such as textiles and weapons were shipped from Europe to Africa, where they were traded for slaves. The slaves were then transported to the Caribbean and North America where they were traded for goods such as sugar, rum, and tobacco. The valuable ships moved along predictable routes and made tempting targets for pirates.

Much of that changed in 1718 when Blackbeard, the most charismatic pirate leader, was killed off the North Carolina coast. It had always been American colonists' greatest fear that the pirates would band together. Their combined forces would have been able to conquer almost any town, and would have been a match for almost any naval

force. After Blackbeard died, though, the Royal Navy made a real effort to kill or capture the remaining pirates. Within a few years, nearly all of Blackbeard's associates were either killed in battle or captured and hanged.

Bartholomew Roberts became a pirate just as the strength of the pirate community was in decline. Though he spent some time around the Caribbean, he changed tactics and began to hit targets off the African coast where he hoped the naval presence wasn't as strong as it was in the Caribbean. Over a period of less than three years he captured more than 400 ships. By many accounts he is considered to be the most skilled pirate who ever sailed the seas. However, he did not get knighted and acquire great wealth like the English-sponsored privateer Henry Morgan. Nor did he get to retire with his fortune like the pirate Henry Every. Instead, like almost every pirate who came before him, he died by violence.

Roberts was an excellent sailor and navigator, and was much more skilled than many of his pirate cohorts. He was also a reluctant pirate. Yet once he made up his mind to pursue his deadly new job, he was a master of his trade. He was sometimes merciful and often cruel. Above all, he was successful.

Black Bart's Pirate Flags

Roberts used at least two different flags during his career as a pirate. His first flag had a black background with two figures in white. One was a man, probably a representation of Roberts himself. The other was a skeleton. Between them they held an hourglass. This let his enemies know that time was running out for them, and their only choice was between surrender and death.

Later, Roberts designed a new flag that showed his bitter hatred of the residents of two Caribbean islands: Martinique and Barbados. The governors of Martinique and Barbados had met

ABH AMH

Roberts with fierce resistance, damaging his ship and killing many of his men. Ever afterward, he had a grudge against people from those two islands, and would be particularly merciless to any residents he captured. His new flag showed him standing on two skulls, one labeled ABH (A Barbadian Head) and the other, AMH (A Martiniquais Head).

two

From Cabin Boy to Captain

The man who would become known as Bartholomew Roberts was born John Roberts, or possibly John Robert, in 1682. His birthplace was Little Newcastle, a village in Pembrokeshire, Wales. His father's name was George Roberts. Young Roberts spoke both Welsh and English. His birthplace and his native language would later prove helpful in launching his career as a pirate.

Roberts probably first went to sea around 1695. Like many other young men, he may have been looking for adventure, or simply a paycheck. He likely signed on as a cabin boy on a merchant ship or a

Most sailors—and pirates—began their careers as cabin boys.

The backstaff (an improvement on the cross-staff) allowed a navigator to find the altitude of the sun, and thus the latitude, without actually facing the sun.

slaver, a ship that carried slaves from Africa to the New World. Even at the age of thirteen, he would have been expected to work very hard while on the ship. At first his duties would be menial. He'd have to perform all the unskilled tasks, leaving the complex jobs such as navigation to the experienced seamen. Roberts would have swabbed the deck, done minor repairs, served the officers, helped in the galley, and run messages up and down the ship.

A Clever Lad

It seems that young Roberts was a clever lad, based on his ability to learn fast and his brazen on-board exploits. If a cabin boy was clever, he would soon begin to collect bits of sailing lore. He'd learn to tie the many knots a sailor needs. He'd learn the intricacies of setting the **rigging**, which was no easy task, since there were dozens of such lines that controlled the sails. He'd get the knack of reading the wind and the currents. Some ships even had formal schooling, with the captain or first mate instructing the cabin boys in reading and arithmetic.

The cleverest of cabin boys might even learn that science was the key to the magic of navigation. Finding one's location on Earth was an inexact practice in the seventeenth century. A variety of methods were used to get from one place to another, and success depended on the ship navigator's experience and skill. On a very basic level, just looking at the stars could give a hint of location and direction. Nearly every sailor would recognize Polaris, the North Star. Those with more advanced knowledge could use a variety of instruments, such as an **astrolabe**, cross-staff or back-staff. These tools let them determine **latitude**, or the measure of how far north or south of the **Equator** they might be.

The real challenge in the seventeenth and eighteenth centuries was how to determine **longitude**, or how far east or west of the **prime meridian** a ship might be. When Roberts was sailing, longitude was mostly calculated by a system called **dead reckoning**. Dead reckoning involves starting at a known position (such as a port or an island) and then calculating speed and time as the ship travels to estimate the new position. The results weren't always accurate,

The astrolabe, which can measure the altitude of the sun and other stars, was one of the navigational tools Roberts would have mastered.

and any mistakes were magnified as the voyage progressed. A navigator who could reduce those errors was valuable. Roberts seems to have learned to be a skilled navigator.

Captured!

Historians know that Roberts was a mate, or deck officer, on a merchant sloop in 1718. Then his life changed in 1719. Roberts was serving as a third mate on the slave ship *Princess*. Working on a slave ship wasn't considered as prestigious as working on a regular merchant ship. Some sailors objected to the slave trade on moral grounds. Even those who didn't would object to the bad conditions and the smell. The human cargo was packed head-to-foot as tightly as possible. Many of the slaves died on the journey across the Atlantic. No one knows what Roberts thought of the slave trade, but when he had a chance to leave it, he did.

Princess landed at Anomabu (also known as Anomabo and Annamaboe), a town in what is known today as Ghana, a country on the Atlantic coast of West Africa. There the pirate Howell Davis and his two ships, *Royal Rover* and *Royal James*, captured *Princess*. Several of the *Princess* crewmembers were forced to join the pirates. Usually pirates didn't just want men who were big and strong. They also needed men with special skills. Carpenters were prized for their ability to repair ships, as were coopers, who made the watertight barrels that stored food and water aboard a ship. Surgeons, too, were useful in the aftermath of battle. Roberts was none of those things. Still, Davis insisted he join up for two reasons.

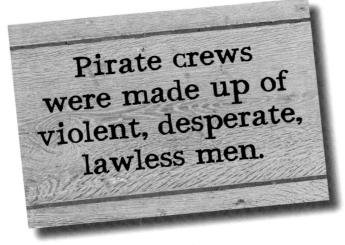

First, the pirate Davis valued Roberts's navigational skills. With his clever mind and years of formal training, Roberts could bring a ship to any point in the sea. He could find even the tiniest islands with accuracy, and track merchant ship targets along trade routes. Perhaps even more than a ship pilot, though, Davis needed an ally.

Pirate crews, by their very nature, were contentious—made up as they were of violent, desperate, lawless men. These pirates might have redeeming qualities—some crewmembers on a pirate ship were educated and even peaceful—but pirates in general were not easy men to control. Davis himself was something of a gentleman pirate. People he had captured noted that he was generous and humane. What Davis really wanted was another gentleman, educated and without particularly bloodthirsty tendencies—one in whom he could confide. Davis grew up in Pembrokeshire, Wales, not far from Roberts's birthplace. The two were countrymen, and both spoke Welsh. Since none of the other crew spoke that language, Davis and Roberts could confer secretly and keep their plans from the other pirates.

It seems that Davis and Roberts became fast friends. The pirate captain trusted his new pilot. Though Roberts was at first reluctant to take to piracy, Davis soon brought him around. Roberts compared the low wages and backbreaking work aboard a slave ship to the liberty, profit, and power he might find as a pirate. Eventually he decided that the only possible drawback might come at the end of his life, if he was captured and hanged. Even that possibility he dismissed, saying it amounted to no more than a "sour look or two at choking." His motto was reputed to be "a merry life and a short one." It was then that he changed his first name from John to Bartholomew.

Roberts's career soon took a brutal turn, however. Just six weeks after Roberts joined his crew, Captain Davis was ambushed and murdered.

The pirate captain Howell Davis and Roberts became friends and allies.

Dancing the Hempen Jig

Not many people were able to retire from a life of piracy. A pirate usually died as he lived: violently. Roberts was no different. Indeed, he assumed from the beginning that he would probably be captured and executed. In the eighteenth century, the penalty for piracy was hanging.

There are several methods of execution by hanging. By the nineteenth century, a scientific system using a drop of between 4 and 6 feet (1.2 to 1.8 meters) that would almost always break the criminal's neck, was put in place. In Roberts's time, most criminals were killed by what is known as the short drop. The prisoner was usually carried to the gallows in a cart, and sometimes permitted to make a final speech. Then the rope was looped around their neck, and the horses pulling the cart were urged forward, leaving the criminal dangling. Death from strangulation might take as much as twenty minutes. It was not a pretty end. Some prisoners would try to leap from the cart, hoping to snap their necks and avoid lingering in misery.

Though hangings later became quicker and more merciful, during the seventeenth and eighteenth centuries the condemned slowly strangled instead of having their necks broken.

In most of the executions a rope made of hemp was used. Some lucky felons got a rope made from silk. Silk ropes were supposed to cinch more tightly and make death come faster. Usually only noblemen got a silk hangman's rope.

Many notorious pirates were captured, tried, and hanged, including Stede Bonnet, Calico Jack Rackham, and William Kidd.

three

The Most Successful Pirate in History

For a few weeks after being pressed into piracy, Roberts participated with the rest of the crew. He proved himself an able navigator and a skilled fighter. They took a few ships, and Roberts was impressed with how easy it was for a pirate to make a fortune. When one of Davis's ships, *Royal James*, had to be abandoned, the entire crew boarded the *Royal Rover* and headed to the island of Príncipe off the west coast of Africa. Davis, who always had a trick up his sleeve, hoisted stolen British navy flags and was welcomed into the harbor. After buying supplies for the ship, the bold Davis invited the local governor

As soon as he became a pirate, Roberts helped his new captain capture several valuable ships.

Shortly after Roberts became a pirate, his new captain was killed in an ambush.

aboard to have lunch. Davis planned to hold the governor hostage for a large ransom, but the governor had been tipped off to Davis's real identity. He accepted the invitation but insisted that Davis first stop by the fort for a glass of wine. The unsuspecting Davis did, and he and his entire party, except for a sailor named Walter Kennedy, were slaughtered.

Roberts was luckily among the pirates still aboard the *Royal Rover*. With the pirates now leaderless, a new captain had to be elected. Though he had only been with the crew for about six weeks at that point, it was decided that Roberts was the best choice. This was probably largely based on his navigational skills, but also because he was reputed to have a very domineering personality. Although an amateur as far as pirates go, he was a natural leader and never afraid to speak his mind. Roberts supposedly said that as long as he had to be a pirate, "It was better to be a pirate captain than a common swabbie," meaning a common seaman who washed the decks.

First Revenge, Then Profit

Roberts's first act was to get bloody revenge on the entire island of Príncipe. With ruthless efficiency, he led the pirates in storming the island, where they slaughtered almost every male resident and stole everything of value. His ship swollen with wealth, Roberts now had a real taste for piracy. In the next few days they captured two big ships. He then called for a vote about where to strike next. The crew voted for the waters off Brazil.

The crew crossed the Atlantic without incident, but once they reached Brazil they couldn't find a single ship for more than two months. Roberts was just about to give up when they discovered a fleet of forty-two Portuguese treasure ships. Bound for Lisbon, Portugal, they were completely unguarded, waiting for two warships to escort them home. Roberts pounced on the nearest ship and ordered the terrified captain to tell him which ship was the richest in the fleet. They knew they would only have time for one strike before the warships came. When the captain pointed out the best ship, Roberts boarded it, and his delighted crew sailed away with thousands of gold coins and precious jewels intended for the king of Portugal.

The huge amount of treasure Roberts easily captured from a Portuguese treasure ship made him very popular with his new crew.

The pirates made merry, spending their loot within a few weeks before they set out to find more. Roberts took a sloop, which he kept as a second pirate ship. Not long after, he spied a tempting brigantine, or two-masted ship. Roberts took half of the pirates in the new sloop and gave chase, leaving the Irish pirate Walter Kennedy in charge of the *Royal Rover*. Kennedy had been with Davis during the fatal ambush, and was the only member of the team to survive, a fact that might have raised suspicions. Was he just lucky, or a traitor who had caused Davis and the other crew members' deaths?

Roberts's sloop was stuck in calm winds for more than a week. By the time he made it back to meet up with Kennedy, he found that the traitor had sailed off with the rest of the crew and the rest of their loot. Roberts then made two vows: He would never again sail with any Irishman, and from that day forward, all pirates under his command would swear on a Bible to abide by a new set of rules which came to be known as the **Pirate Code**. He renamed his ship the *Fortune*, and resumed piracy.

Roberts became known for his code—and for his capacity for revenge. In February 1720, Roberts experienced bad luck when the governor of the island of Barbados sent two well-armed sloops after him. Though he escaped, his ship was crippled and twenty of his men were killed. Not long afterward, the governor of Martinique sent more ships after the already-weakened pirate captain. As his ship limped to safety, Roberts swore vengeance against every resident of Barbados and Martinique. He had a new flag made, showing him standing on skulls of residents of those islands. From then on, though he was sometimes merciful to those he captured, he was never merciful to people from Barbados or Martinique.

Thereafter, Roberts went on a regular spree of piracy, capturing, looting, and burning scores of ships. He ranged as far north as Newfoundland in modern-day Canada, where he was so fearsome that every captain and crew in the harbor abandoned their ships when facing him. Roberts captured twenty-two vessels simply by flying his fearsome flag. In his entire career he captured, or intimidated into paying him, more than 470 ships.

Black Bart's Pirate Code

To help keep his crew in line, Roberts decided to spell out the rules and regulations, prizes and penalties for every member of his ship. This list, called the "Articles of Agreement," was known as the Pirate Code. Every pirate who served under Roberts had to swear to follow his laws.

After living under the dictatorship of merchant captains, Roberts wanted something closer to democracy aboard his ship. His first article stated: "Every man shall have an equal vote in affairs of moment." He then promised everyone would have a fair share of food and "strong liquor."

Next in order of importance were money matters. Each man's share was determined by his rank and position, with the captain and **quartermaster** getting two shares, the master gunner and boatswain getting one and one half shares, other officers one and one quarter, and regular pirates one share each. If anyone took a single coin more than they were owed, they would be marooned, or abandoned on a desert island or isolated shore.

To avoid conflicts, no gambling was allowed. Women, too, were forbidden aboard his ship, in case romantic jealousy led to a duel.

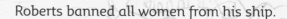
Fighting on the ship was forbidden. "None shall strike another on board the ship, but every man's quarrel shall be ended on shore by sword or pistol in this manner."

Safety and readiness were also among Roberts's concerns. Lights had to be out by 8 p.m., partly to keep the ship from being easily spotted at night, but also to keep the men (who might well be intoxicated at night) from setting fire to the ship's belowdeck area where the highly flammable gunpowder was stored. Also, the crew were instructed to keep their blades sharp and their pistols clean and ready for a fight at all times. Any man who showed cowardice in battle would either be killed or marooned on an island.

To make sure his crew didn't abandon their piratical life too soon, they had to swear not to leave until they had made a certain amount of money. Roberts also provided a kind of insurance, saying, "Every man who shall become a cripple or lose a limb in the service shall have 800 pieces of eight from the common stock and for lesser hurts proportionately."

The Man Behind the Pirate

What kind of man was Roberts? He was a man of many contradictions. He had no desire to be a pirate, but when he was forced to take it up, he excelled. Unlike most of his cohorts, he was reputed to be a **teetotaler**, preferring hot tea with lemon to rum and grog. He might have even been religious, for he made a point of letting his ship musicians rest on the Sabbath. He was a handsome man with dark hair and flashing eyes, who loved to dress well. He would adorn himself with the fine clothes and precious jewelry stolen from the ships he captured. Roberts was definitely educated, and is sometimes described as a gentleman.

Despite his refined exterior, Roberts was capable of shocking violence. For example, in 1720 he came upon a man-of-war ship that had the governor of Martinique on board. Roberts pretended to be a French merchant vessel and approached the ship, promising to give the governor news of his enemy: the pirate Bartholomew Roberts. Once Roberts and his crew were close enough, they sprayed the man-of-war with cannonballs and pistol fire, and captured the governor of Martinique. Roberts dragged him to his ship and immediately hung him from the yardarm. According to some stories, he let his corpse swing there until it rotted while seabirds plucked at its eyes. Roberts clearly hadn't forgotten his deadly grudge against everyone from Martinique.

It seems that Roberts often tempered his actions to the whims of his crew. A captain may want to be merciful, but if his crew is calling for

Bartholomew Roberts doodgebleeven.

In many ways, Roberts was an enigma, part gentleman, part ruthless buccaneer.

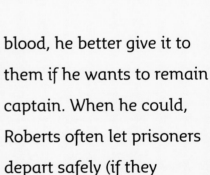

blood, he better give it to them if he wants to remain captain. When he could, Roberts often let prisoners depart safely (if they weren't from Ireland, Martinique, or Barbados). He would even give them gifts from previously looted ships. However, if his crewmen were feeling restless and violent, Roberts would let them torture prisoners in cruel ways. He knew that if he didn't keep his pirates happy, they'd mutiny, which meant they'd overthrow him and elect a new captain.

four

The End of Black Bart

From 1720 to 1721, Roberts was so active in the Caribbean that he almost single-handedly stopped maritime trade in the region. He took almost every ship that dared to enter what he considered to be *his* waters. Eventually, trade ships simply stopped sailing in the region. It was too dangerous. When there was nothing left to pillage, Roberts decided to cross back across the Atlantic and raid along the African coast.

In June 1721, Roberts had reached the Guinea coast. Two French ships tried to attack him, but he beat them easily and took the vessels for his own use. Now he sailed with his flagship the *Royal Fortune*, and his new

Wooden ships deteriorated easily in tropical waters, and had to be periodically beached and repaired, a process known as careening.

Once Black Bart's ravages shut down all trade in the Caribbean, he tried his luck off the African coast.

ships *Ranger* and *Little Ranger*. Roberts heard a rumor that the two biggest British warships in the region, the HMS *Weymouth* and the HMS *Swallow*, had left the area and wouldn't return until Christmas. This meant Roberts and his men were free to attack every ship along the coast.

In November and December of 1721, Roberts took some time off. His ships were in need of repair, so he **careened** them on an island. This meant that the ships were brought as far onto the beach as possible at high tide, and hauled to their sides so the crew could repair damage below the waterline. Barnacles and several kinds of boring mollusks (often called shipworms) would eat away at the wooden hulls of ships. Such creatures had to be scraped off, and wood had to be replaced periodically and treated with tar to keep the ship seaworthy.

After that, though Roberts knew that the British warships would be cruising local waters again, he resumed attacking ships in January 1722. It was during this time that Roberts landed at Whydah, where he set fire to the slave ship *Porcupine* because its captain refused to pay him off. Most of the eighty slaves onboard were still chained. It was Roberts's most cruel act, and one of his last.

The HMS *Swallow* Swoops In

Captain Chaloner Ogle was knighted for his role in taking down the pirate Bartholomew Roberts.

On February 5, 1772, the HMS *Swallow*, captained by Chaloner Ogle, came upon all three of Roberts's ships on Cape Lopez, a long, narrow peninsula on the coast of what is now Gabon. Probably two of Roberts's ships were careened. As the *Swallow* approached the three ships, one of two things happened. Either the pilot had to suddenly veer to avoid a **shoal**, or the captain ordered a clever maneuver to lure one of the pirate ships away from the others.

In either case, the result was that one of Roberts's ships, the *Ranger*, thought the *Swallow* was a fleeing merchant ship and set sails in pursuit.

The swift *Swallow* led the *Ranger* around the cape and away until it was out of hearing range of the rest of the pirates. Then it opened fire, with devastating results. Ten of the crewmembers were killed. The *Ranger*'s captain, James Skyrme, had his leg blown off by a cannonball. Refusing to surrender, he bled to death. Upon his death, the *Ranger* surrendered and all the surviving pirates were captured.

Pirate Cannons

Cannons were the primary weapons in ship-to-ship warfare. Though small arms and edged weapons were useful after boarding an enemy ship, the main battle was often decided by cannon fire. Most pirate cannons shot balls of 32 pounds (14.5 kg) or less, but the cannons themselves could weigh more than 3,000 pounds (1,361 kg), or the weight of the average car!

Firing a cannon was a multi-step process. The barrel had to be swabbed with a damp cloth to put out any sparks from the last firing. Then gunpowder, cloth packing, and the cannonball itself was rammed into the barrel. Then finer gunpowder was added to the breech, or back end of the cannon. When given the command, a pirate would light the gunpowder, shooting the cannonball out the other end. When the gun recoiled, it could jump back several feet, and crewmembers had to be careful not to be crushed. Some sailors could—and often did—lose a limb just from the recoil of a cannon.

Though it took lots of time, gunpowder, and men to fire a cannon, the results were devastating. A single cannonball could take down a mast or punch a hole below the waterline. However, most pirates did not, in fact, try to sink the ships they were attacking. Not only were the ships themselves valuable, but sinking a ship also meant sending all of its valuable cargo down with it!

Roberts didn't seem concerned about the *Ranger*'s disappearance. The sea is an uncertain place, and he likely assumed the ship had put in for repairs, or chased another prize, or any of a dozen possibilities. While they were waiting, Roberts captured a passing ship called the *Neptune*, and his men were drinking the alcohol they had found among the cargo. When they spied sails on February 10, 1772, they assumed it was the *Ranger* returning. One of the crew, who had in fact deserted from the *Swallow* some months before, soon recognized the ship, however. Roberts prepared for battle.

Dressed For the Occasion

Roberts rose in leisurely fashion from the breakfast he had been sharing with the *Neptune*'s captured captain, and dressed in his finest suit of bright, blood-red cloth. He put a red feather in his hat, and hung a gold chain with a diamond cross around his neck. Then, arming himself with his sword and four pistols strapped across his body, he commanded his ship to sail past the *Swallow*.

Roberts was confident as ever. The man who had taken more than 400 ships and evaded the Royal Navy for years was not about to fear any ship, even a man-of-war vessel such as the *Swallow*. However, knowing that his crew was drunk, he decided to flee rather than fight. He'd only have to expose his ship to one broadside, or volley of cannon fire from the *Swallow*, and then his ship could escape to open waters.

Roberts's crew was intoxicated and unable to fight effectively when the HMS *Swallow* launched her attack.

There was one problem with the plan. The crewman at the helm, still under the influence of liquor, couldn't keep the *Royal Fortune* on course. The ship slowed and turned, allowing the formidable *Swallow* to deliver another deadly broadside.

There would be no slow trial and agonizing strangulation at the end of a hemp rope for Roberts. Nor would there be a last dramatic battle, man to man with his foe. Among the cannonballs, the *Swallow* launched a round of many small cannonballs, called grapeshot, that pierced Roberts in the throat as he stood defiantly on deck. The man who all the pirates had called "pistol proof" was able to be hurt after all. Bartholomew Roberts collapsed. He died instantly.

The Aftermath

Roberts had always said that if he died in battle, he didn't want his body to be taken by the enemy. He knew they would display his corpse in an undignified way. As soon as he was killed, his crew hastily wrapped his body in a ship's sail, weighted it down, and tossed it overboard.

The sailor had returned to the sea. His body was never found.

The fight went on for another two hours, but Roberts's crew never had a chance. Without their valiant leader, the other pirates soon surrendered. One of Roberts's loyal crew tried to blow up the ship, but other crewmembers who had been forced into piracy stopped him. All told, the *Swallow* captured 272 pirates. Only three pirates were killed in the battle.

Of those captured, fifty-two were hanged. Another twenty were allowed to sell themselves as **indentured servants** to the Royal African Company, which would have involved working in Africa in the slave trade or hunting for gold, and might just mean a slower death. Sixty-five pirates were black; they were sold into slavery. More than a third of the pirates were found not guilty and released. Some of those men had probably been forced into piracy when their ships were captured. Captain Ogle received a knighthood, and also kept all of the gold he discovered in Roberts's private cabin.

After his death, the people who wrote about Roberts named him "Black Bart," and this name has lived in infamy through the centuries. He is mentioned in one of the most famous pirate novels of all time, Robert Louis Stevenson's *Treasure Island*. He was also the inspiration for the Dread Pirate Roberts in the beloved novel and movie, *The Princess Bride*. Roberts even makes appearances in Disney's *Pirates of the Caribbean* and several pirate-themed video games. Though his criminal career was cut short, the reluctant pirate Captain Roberts earned his place among the top pirates in history.

Timeline

1682 Bartholomew Roberts (originally named John Roberts) is born in Wales.

1695 Roberts goes to sea for the first time, probably as a cabin boy.

1718 Roberts serves as a mate on a sloop sailing out of Barbados.

1718 The pirate Blackbeard is killed off the North Carolina coast, signaling increased naval opposition to piracy.

1719 Roberts's ship is captured by pirate captain Howell Davis; Roberts is forced to join the crew.

1720 Ships from Barbados and Martinique pursue Roberts, damaging his ships and killing crewmembers. This leads to Roberts's lifelong hatred of residents of those islands.

1720	Roberts captures the governor of Martinique, whom he executes and hangs from the ship's yardarm.
1720	Roberts's raids in the Caribbean are so damaging that trade virtually stops.
1721	Roberts takes his ships to the African coast.
1722	In January, Roberts sets fire to the slave ship *Porcupine*, without first freeing the majority of the eighty slaves aboard.
1722	On Feburary 10, Roberts is killed by grapeshot fired from the HMS *Swallow*, captained by Chaloner Ogle.

Though his crew believed he was indestructible, Roberts was felled by a spray of deadly grape shot off the coast of Africa.

Glossary

astrolabe An instrument used to determine the altitude of the sun and other stars; used for science or navigation.

careen To turn a ship on its side for cleaning, caulking, or repair.

dead reckoning Determining position based on knowledge of a previous point, and the speed and time at which one travels away from that point.

Equator An imaginary line drawn around the Earth equally distant from both poles, dividing the Earth into northern and southern hemispheres.

Golden Age of Piracy The period from the 1650s to the 1730s when piracy flourished in the Caribbean, Atlantic Ocean, and elsewhere.

indentured servant A person who has sold themselves into debt bondage for a fixed number of years.

latitude The distance north or south of the equator.

longitude The distance east or west of the prime meridian.

pillage To rob or loot a place, especially with violence or during war.

pirate A person who, without authorization, attacks and plunders ships, or attacks the land from the sea.

Pirate Code Also known as the Articles of Agreement, the set of rules set out by a pirate captain and agreed upon by all of the crew, governing behavior and division of spoils.

pragmatist A person who is practical and goal oriented, who does not let emotion interfere with their judgment but rather relies on logic.

prime meridian Earth's zero of longitude, which by convention passes through Greenwich, England. Also known as the Greenwich meridian.

privateer A person authorized by a government to attack and plunder ships and towns of an enemy nation.

quartermaster The officer (or pirate) aboard a ship responsible for such provisions as food and clothing for the crew; on a pirate ship, the quartermaster usually regulates the division of treasure.

rigging The system of ropes, tackle, and chains that is used to support and control the sails, masts, and other parts of a sailing ship.

shoal A sandbank, sandbar, or other place where the water is shallow.

teetotaler A person who does not drink any alcohol.

triangular slave trade The system of trade from the late seventeenth to the early nineteenth century where manufactured goods were shipped from Europe to Africa and then traded for slaves, who were then shipped to the Americas where they were traded for raw materials such as sugar and tobacco.

Find Out More

Books

Beahm, George. *Caribbean Pirates: A Treasure Chest of Fact, Fiction, and Folklore.* Charlottesville, VA: Hampton Roads Publishing, 2007.

Hamilton, Sue. *Pirates: Bartholomew Roberts.* Edina, MN: ABDO Publishing, 2007.

Platt, Richard. *Pirate Diary: The Journal of Jake Carpenter.* Somerville, MA: Candlewick Press, 2005.

Steer, Dugald A., and Lubber, Captain William. *Pirateology.* Somerville, MA: Candlewick Press, 2006.

Websites

The Crimson Pirate

www.thecrimsonpirate.com/crimsonpirate.us

Explore the history of piracy dating back to more than 3,000 years. Learn about their lives at sea and on land, myths and punishments, view their photos, and read their individual bios.

Gentlemen of Fortune

www.gentlemenoffortune.com/index.htm

Reenact the life of a pirate! Find information about historical clothing and equipment for late seventeenth and early eighteenth century seamen. Discover their weapons, lifestyle, and learn more about their ships.

Museums

The New England Pirate Museum

www.piratemuseum.com/pirate.html

Located in Salem, Massachusetts, this museum features a walking tour through the world of pirates, including recreations of a dockside village, ship, and a cave. Also on display are authentic pirate treasures.

The Pirates of Nassau

www.pirates-of-nassau.com/home.htm

Nassau was a pirate sanctuary for many years, welcoming Black Bart and many other noted pirates. This museum, located in the Bahamas, celebrates their exciting history.

The Queen Anne's Revenge Lab

www.qaronline.org

The researchers at the East Carolina University's West Research Campus in Greenville, North Carolina, have spent years collecting and analyzing artifacts from Blackbeard's famous flagship, *The Queen Anne's Revenge*, which sank just before Roberts was active. The artifacts are similar to items that would have been on Roberts's ships. The lab offers occasional tours, open houses, and traveling exhibits.

The St. Augustine Pirate and Treasure Museum

www.thepiratemuseum.com

This interactive museum covers 300 years of pirate history, and boasts many artifacts including pirate loot, a real treasure chest, and one of only three surviving Jolly Roger flags.

Bibliography

Beahm, George. *Caribbean Pirates: A Treasure Chest of Fact, Fiction, and Folklore.* Charlottesville, VA: Hampton Roads Publishing, 2007.

Cordingly, David. *Under the Black Flag: The Romance and Reality of Life Among the Pirates.* New York, NY: Random House, 1995.

Johnson, Captain Charles. *A General History of the Robberies and Murders of the Most Notorious Pyrates.* London, England: Nathaniel Mist, 1724.

Klein, Shelley. *The Most Evil Pirates in History.* London, England: Michael O'Mara Books, 2006.

Konstam, Angus and Kean, Roger Michael. *Pirates: Predators of the Seas.* New York, NY: Skyhorse Publishing, 2007.

Sanders, Richard. *If a Pirate I Must Be—The True Story of Black Bart, King of the Caribbean Pirates.* New York, NY: Skyhorse Publishing, 2007.

Index

Page numbers in **boldface** are illustrations.

Blackbeard, 8–10
British navy, 7, 23
    see also Royal Navy

Davis, Howell, 17–18, **19**, 23–24, 26

Fortune, the, 27

Golden Age of Piracy, the, 8–9

hanging, 20–21
HMS *Swallow*, the, 34–35, 37–39
HMS *Weymouth*, the, 34

Kennedy, Walter, 24, 26–27

Ogle, Captain Chaloner, **35**, 39

Pirate Code, 27–29
Porcupine, the, 6–7, 35

Ranger, the, 34–35, 37
Roberts, Black Bart (Bartholomew) (John),
    and Barbados, 11, 27, 31
    and Martinique, 11, 27, 30–31
    as a navigator, 10, **14**, 15–16, 23
    capture into piracy, 16–18
    death, 38–39
    early life, 13–16
    nickname origin, 8
    success as a pirate, 23–31
Royal Fortune, the, 33–34, 38
Royal James, the, 17, 23
Royal Rover, the, 17, 23–24, 26
Royal Navy, 9, 10, 37

Skyrme, James, 35

triangular slave trade, 9

About the Author

Laura L. Sullivan is a prolific author of books for children and young adults. Her novels include the fantasies *Under the Green Hill* and *Guardian of the Green Hill*, as well as the historical novels *Ladies in Waiting* and *Love by the Morning Star*. She is also the author of *Sir Henry Morgan* and *Blackbeard* for Cavendish Square's True-Life Pirates series. She lives on the west coast of Florida, where she searches for buried treasure (even though she knows that pirates almost never buried their booty).